BASIC FIDDLE

philharmonic
CELTIC FIDDLE TUNES

andrew h. dabczynski & bob phillips

Welcome to *Basic Fiddlers Philharmonic: Celtic Fiddle Tunes*

Alfred's *Fiddlers Philharmonic* series has developed out of a love for fiddle music in all its many forms and styles. *Basic Fiddlers Philharmonic: Celtic Fiddle Tunes* presents a set of tunes that sound great with beginning string players. These Celtic Fiddle Tunes have roots in Irish, Scottish, Welsh, and Irish-American folk music, as well as 19th-century popular music. They often can be sung with fun and easy words. With *Basic Fiddlers Philharmonic: Celtic Fiddle Tunes*, beginning string players will develop critical string-playing skills, and also learn how to improvise, arrange, and create satisfying musical presentations both alone and with friends. Students with various levels of ability can learn the tunes and play them together using the unique and effective *Fiddlers Philharmonic* format. Students can play along wth the recording.

Following some historical background, each tune is presented in a basic, simplified version intended for the beginning player. Where appropriate, words are provided so students can sing along. A more advanced version of the tune appears next, with some musical variations that are designed to challenge and motivate students. A back-up part is then provided where students can improvise simple accompanying harmonies and rhythms using the printed parts as a departure point. All parts can be played together in any combination. The last page of the book provides students with additional simple-but-effective ideas for fiddling improvisation. More information, ideas for teachers, and piano accompaniments are included elsewhere in the comprehensive Teacher's Score.

So rosin up the bow, dive in, and have fun with *Basic Fiddlers Philharmonic: Celtic Fiddle Tunes!*

CONTENTS

Alfred Music Publishing Co., Inc.
16320 Roscoe Blvd., Suite 100
P.O. Box 10003
Van Nuys, CA 91410-0003
alfred.com

HIGHLAND/ETLING
A DIVISION OF **Alfred**

Copyright © 2009 by Alfred Music Publishing Co., Inc.
All rights reserved.Printed in USA.
ISBN-10: 0-7390-6236-0 (Book)
ISBN-13: 978-0-7390-6236-4
ISBN-10: 0-7390-6237-9 (Book and CD)
ISBN-13: 978-0-6237-4857-1

Rakes of Mallow

The "Rakes of Mallow" is such a well-known tune that it is often considered a "standard" among Irish fiddle players. Like most fiddle tunes, no one knows exactly who composed it—or when—but it first appeared in tune collections before 1750. It was originally a tavern song, and is known by other titles. Those titles include "The Galway Piper" and "Piping Tim," with fun words about the town piper (flute or whistle player).

Lyrics

Ev'ry person in the nation
Whether great or humble station
Holds in highest estimation
Piping Tim of Galway.
Loudly can he play high or low,
He can move you fast or slow,
Touch your hearts or stir your toe
Piping Tim of Galway.

*(A reproducible vocal lead sheet is
included in the Teacher's Score)*

Basic Tune

Track 2

Lively (♩ = 130)

Irish Reel

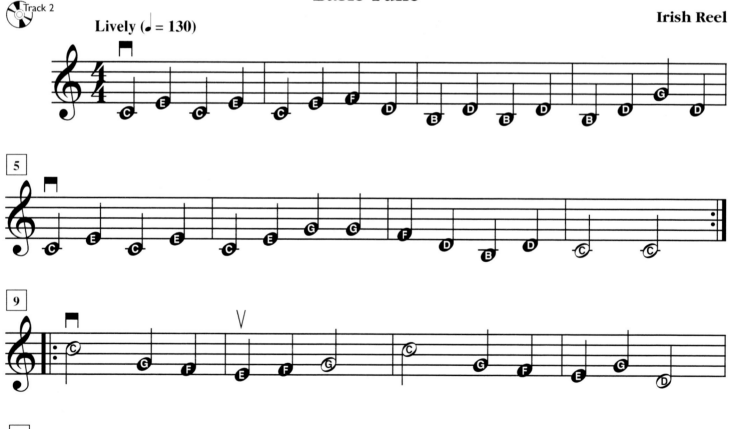

Rakes of Mallow

Advanced Tune

Irish Reel

Improvised back-up — On your own, try making up a rhythm pattern and deciding what notes to play (choose from the printed notes, or talk with your teacher about using other chord tones).

John Ryan's Polka

During the 19th century, a dance called the *polka* became popular throughout Europe,
the United States, and in many other places in the world, including Ireland. Many energetic,
toe-tapping tunes—always in 2/4 time—have been composed so dancers can polka!
One of these is "John Ryan's Polka," a tune probably written by a musician of that name,
that has become a favorite wherever Celtic polkas are played.

Basic Tune

Track 5

Irish Polka

Lively (♩ = 140)

John Ryan's Polka

Advanced Tune

Track 6

Lively (♩ = 140)

Irish Polka

Back-up Directions

Basic back-up — play the notes in each measure as printed.

Regular back-up — play the notes in each measure using the Shuffle Pattern.

Advanced back-up — play the notes in each measure using the On/Off Pattern.

Shuffle Pattern

On/Off Pattern

Back-up Part

Track 7

Lively (♩ = 140)

Improvised back-up — On your own, try making up a rhythm pattern and deciding what notes to play
(choose from the printed notes, or talk with your teacher about using other chord tones).

Skye Boat Song

The "Skye Boat Song" tells a famous story in Scottish history. It describes the escape of Bonnie Prince Charlie after his army of Scottish Highlanders was defeated by the British in 1746 at the Battle of Culloden. Dressed as a maid, and with the help of Scottish heroine Flora MacDonald, he escaped to the Isle of Skye in a small boat. Over a century later, Sir Harold Boulton wrote poetry about that event that was then set to an old Scottish *air*, or melody. Today, the expressive melody is usually played rather slowly and with feeling.

Lyrics

Chorus:
Speed, bonnie boat, like a bird on the wing,
Onward! the sailors cry;
Carry the lad that's born to be King
Over the sea to Skye.

1. Loud the winds howl, loud the waves roar,
Thunderclaps rend the air;
Baffled, our foes stand by the shore,
Follow they will not dare.
Chorus

(A reproducible vocal lead sheet is included in the Teacher's Score)

2. Though the waves leap, soft shall ye sleep,
Ocean's a royal bed.
Rocked in the deep, Flora will keep
Watch by your weary head.
Chorus

3. Many's the lad fought on that day,
Well the Claymore could wield,
When the night came, silently lay
Dead in Culloden's field.
Chorus

4. Burned are their homes, exile and death
Scatter the loyal men;
Yet ere the sword cool in the sheath
Charlie will come again.
Chorus

Basic Tune

Track 8

Scottish Air

Skye Boat Song

Advanced Tune

Scottish Air

Back-up Directions
Basic back-up — play the notes in each measure as printed.
Regular back-up — play the notes in each measure using the Shuffle Pattern.
Advanced back-up — play the notes in each measure using the On/Off Pattern.

Back-up Part

Improvised back-up — On your own, try making up a rhythm pattern and deciding what notes to play
(choose from the printed notes, or talk with your teacher about using other chord tones).

The Girl I Left Behind Me

Like many Celtic fiddle tunes, no one is exactly sure where "The Girl I Left Behind Me" was composed. Whether it is from Britain or Ireland is unsure, but it has been played since before 1700. The tune became a popular *reel* for dancing in America, and also was sung and used as a march by armies in the Revolutionary War, the War of 1812, and the Civil War. The song's words reflect the feelings of soldiers who leave loved ones behind.

Lyrics

1. The hours sad I left a maid
   A lingering farewell taking
   Whose sighs and tears my steps delayed
   I thought her heart was breaking
   In hurried words her name I blest
   I breathed the vows that bind me
   And to my heart in anguish pressed
   The girl I left behind me.

2. Then to the east we bore away
   To win a name in story
   And there where dawns the sun of day
   There dawned our sun of glory
   The place in my sight
   When in the host assigned me
   I shared the glory of that fight
   Sweet girl I left behind me.

3. Though many a name our banner bore
   Of former deeds of daring
   But they were of the day of yore
   In which we had no sharing
   But now our laurels freshly won
   With the old one shall entwine me
   Singing worthy of our size each son
   Sweet girl I left behind me.

4. The hope of final victory
   Within my bosom burning
   Is mingling with sweet thoughts of thee
   And of my fond returning
   But should I n'eer return again
   Still with thy love i'll bind me
   Dishonors breath shall never stain
   The name I leave behind me.

(A reproducible vocal lead sheet is included in the Teacher's Score)

Basic Tune

Track 11

Lively (♩ = 130)

Irish Reel

The Girl I Left Behind Me

Advanced Tune

Irish Reel

Back-up Directions
Basic back-up — play the notes in each measure as printed.
Regular back-up — play the notes in each measure using the Shuffle Pattern.
Advanced back-up — play the notes in each measure using the On/Off Pattern.

Improvised back-up — On your own, try making up a rhythm pattern and deciding what notes to play
(choose from the printed notes, or talk with your teacher about using other chord tones).

The Minstrel Boy

It is said that the well known Irish poet and singer Thomas More (1779–1852) lost a number of close friends in the 1798 Irish Rebellion against British rule. In their memory, he wrote a lovely poem titled "The Minstrel Boy" that described a brave minstrel—a musician such as his friends and himself— who dies in battle. He set the poem to a familiar old Irish tune known as "The Moreen." Thomas More often sang it, and it became very popular both in Ireland and the United States, both as a song and as a slow, expressive fiddle *air.*

Lyrics

1. The Minstrel Boy to the war is gone
   In the ranks of death you will find him;
   His father's sword he hath girded on,
   And his wild harp slung behind him;
   "Land of Song!" said the warrior bard,
   "Tho' all the world betrays thee,
   One sword, at least, thy rights shall guard,
   One faithful harp shall praise thee!"

2. The Minstrel fell! But the foreman's chain
   Could not bring that proud soul under;
   The harp he lov'd ne'er spoke again,
   For he tore its chords asunder;
   And said "No chains shall sully thee,
   Thou soul of love and brav'ry!
   Thy songs were made for the pure and free,
   They shall never sound in slavery!"

(A reproducible vocal lead sheet is included in the Teacher's Score)

Basic Tune

The Minstrel Boy

Advanced Tune

Irish Air

Back-up Directions
Basic back-up — play the notes in each measure as printed.
Regular back-up — play the notes in each measure using the Shuffle Pattern.
Advanced back-up — play the notes in each measure using the On/Off Pattern.

Shuffle Pattern

On/Off Pattern

Back-up Part

Improvised back-up — On your own, try making up a rhythm pattern and deciding what notes to play
(choose from the printed notes, or talk with your teacher about using other chord tones).

The Wind That Shakes the Barley

"The Wind That Shakes the Barley" is usually considered to be an Irish reel, though probably it is of Scottish origin. It is difficult to know when the tune was composed, but we know it was played in the mid-1800s, and ever since, has been a favorite wherever Celtic music is popular. Many sets of words have been set to "The Wind That Shakes the Barley," and one is included here. See if the movement that can be heard in the melody and rhythm of the tune seem like the constantly shifting patterns that occur when wind passes over fields of barley wheat.

Lyrics
Oh, won't you rattle me, and oh, won't you chase me,
Oh, won't you rattle me, the little bag of tailors.
Oh, won't you rattle me, and oh, won't you chase me,
Oh, won't you rattle me, the little bag of tailors.

(A reproducible vocal lead sheet is included in the Teacher's Score)

Basic Tune

Track 17

Irish Reel

Lively (♩ = 130)

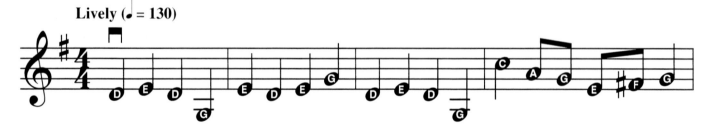

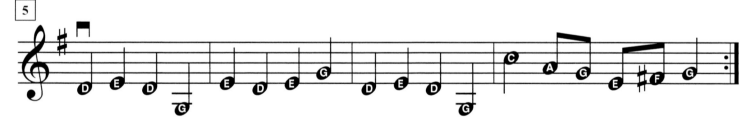

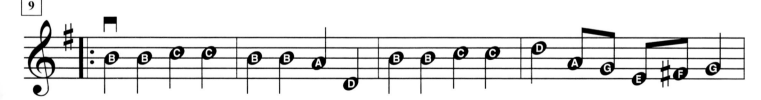

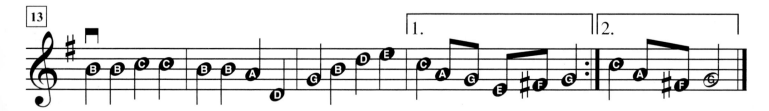

The Wind That Shakes the Barley

Advanced Tune

Irish Reel

Back-up Directions

Basic back-up — play the notes in each measure as printed.

Regular back-up — play the notes in each measure using the Shuffle Pattern.

Advanced back-up — play the notes in each measure using the On/Off Pattern.

Shuffle Pattern

On/Off Pattern

Back-up Part

Improvised back-up — On your own, try making up a rhythm pattern and deciding what notes to play
(choose from the printed notes, or talk with your teacher about using other chord tones).

MacPherson's Lament

A *lament* is a sad-sounding melody written when someone departs or dies. According to legend, "MacPherson's Lament" was composed by one of Scotland's first fiddler-composers, James MacPherson, on the eve of his own execution. It is said that MacPherson was a large and handsome rover, and a fiddler popular in his home area of Banffshire. But the legend says that he became proud and arrogant, and fell in with a band of highwaymen, or robbers. He was caught in 1700 and sentenced to hang. Supposedly, he wrote this lament during his last night in prison, sang and played it the next morning on the gallows as his last communication with the world, then smashed his fiddle in a final act of defiance! Whether or not any of this is true will never be known, but it makes a terrific story!

Lyrics
Farewell, ye dungeons dark and strong,
The wretch's destiny!
MacPherson's time will not be long
On yonder gallows tree.
Sing rantingly, sing wantonly,
Sing dauntingly of he,
He play'd a spring, and danc'd it round
Below the gallows tree.

(A reproducible vocal lead sheet is included in the Teacher's Score)

Basic Tune

Track 20

Slowly (♩ = 80)

Scottish Air

MacPherson's Lament

Advanced Tune

Back-up Directions
Basic back-up — play the notes in each measure as printed.
Regular back-up — play the notes in each measure using the Shuffle Pattern.
Advanced back-up — play the notes in each measure using the On/Off Pattern.

Improvised back-up — On your own, try making up a rhythm pattern and deciding what notes to play
(choose from the printed notes, or talk with your teacher about using other chord tones).

Breakdown Hornpipe

A *hornpipe* is a type of dance, as well as the tune played for that dance, in 4/4 time.
It seems to have originated in the British Isles, perhaps as early as the 16th century, and
is often associated with seafaring. The "Breakdown Hornpipe" is a typical example, with
roots in Scotland. Hornpipes are often played with a bit of a swing or lilt, but can also be
played "straight," like a reel.

Basic Tune

Track 23

Irish Hornpipe

Lilting (♩ = 140)

Breakdown Hornpipe

Advanced Tune

Irish Hornpipe

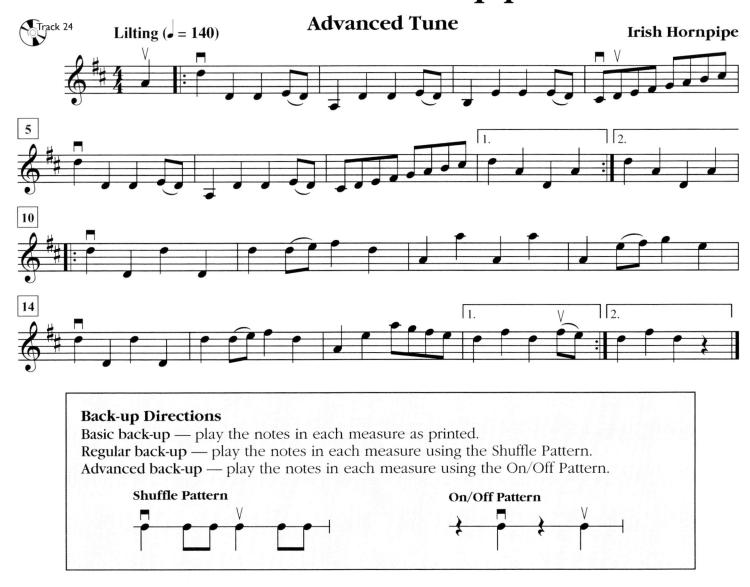

Back-up Directions
Basic back-up — play the notes in each measure as printed.
Regular back-up — play the notes in each measure using the Shuffle Pattern.
Advanced back-up — play the notes in each measure using the On/Off Pattern.

Shuffle Pattern   **On/Off Pattern**

Back-up Part

Improvised back-up — On your own, try making up a rhythm pattern and deciding what notes to play
(choose from the printed notes, or talk with your teacher about using other chord tones).

The Irish Washerwoman

The *jig* is one of the oldest folk dances that has survived to our day. Probably developed in Italy, the jig made its way to Ireland, likely during the Baroque era. Jigs became so popular there that today people think of them as being Irish. "The Irish Washerwoman" is certainly one of the best known of the Irish "simple jigs"—tunes in 6/8 time. It dates back to the early 1600s, and later became popular throughout the British Isles, the United States, Australia, and anywhere else the Irish have taken their music.

Track 26

Basic Tune

Irish Jig

The Irish Washerwoman
Advanced Tune

Irish Jig

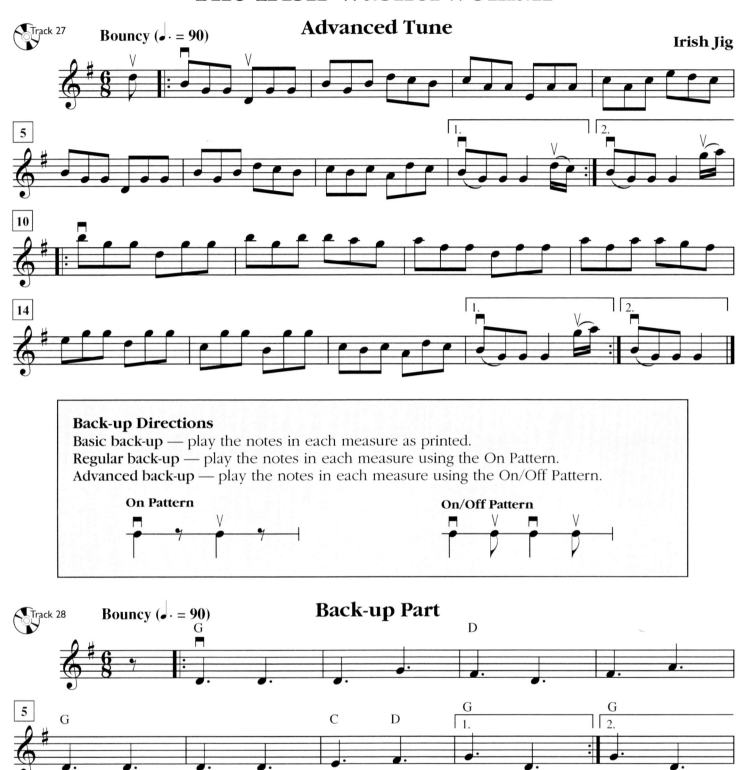

Back-up Directions

Basic back-up — play the notes in each measure as printed.
Regular back-up — play the notes in each measure using the On Pattern.
Advanced back-up — play the notes in each measure using the On/Off Pattern.

On Pattern

On/Off Pattern

Back-up Part

Improvised back-up — On your own, try making up a rhythm pattern and deciding what notes to play
(choose from the printed notes, or talk with your teacher about using other chord tones).

Haste to the Wedding

It is assumed that the origins of "Haste to the Wedding" are Gaelic—that is, Irish. This jig tune was known as early as the late 1700s. It quickly became popular with Irish, Scottish, British, and American fiddlers, and has been ever since. It has been said that in Ireland's County Donegal there was an old tradition that on her wedding day a bride—along with her family and friends—would march from her house to the church, with a fiddler leading the way while playing this jig.

Basic Tune

Track 29

Bouncy (♩. = 90)

Irish Jig

Haste to the Wedding
Advanced Tune

Irish Jig

Back-up Directions
Basic back-up — play the notes in each measure as printed.
Regular back-up — play the notes in each measure using the Shuffle Pattern.
Advanced back-up — play the notes in each measure using the On/Off Pattern.

Shuffle Pattern   **On/Off Pattern**

Back-up Part

Improvised back-up — On your own, try making up a rhythm pattern and deciding what notes to play
(choose from the printed notes, or talk with your teacher about using other chord tones).

Harvest Home Hornpipe

"Harvest Home Hornpipe" has been played by fiddlers for some 200 years. Exactly where it was composed is unknown—maybe Ireland, maybe Britain—but it is now common to hear it played by many Celtic musicians. Sometimes "Harvest Home" is known by other titles, including "Cork Hornpipe," "Cincinnati Hornpipe," and in Irish, "Deire An Fogmair." Like other hornpipes, this tune sounds terrific when it is played with a swinging lilt, but many fiddlers play it like a reel with steady eighth notes.

Track 32

Basic Tune

Scottish Hornpipe

Harvest Home Hornpipe

Advanced Tune

Scottish Hornpipe

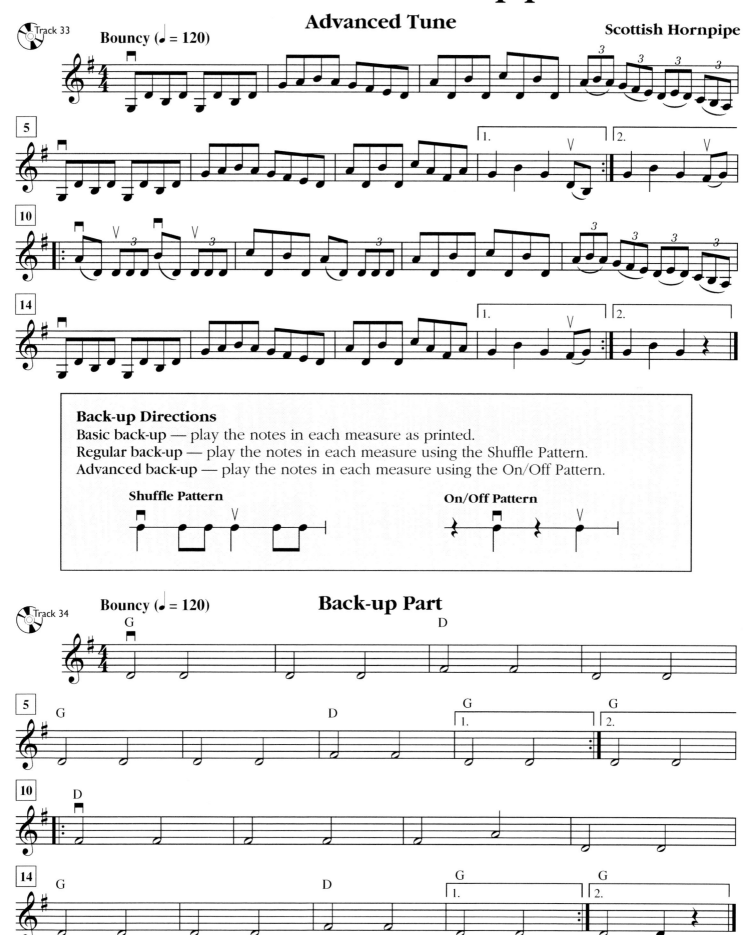

Back-up Directions

Basic back-up — play the notes in each measure as printed.
Regular back-up — play the notes in each measure using the Shuffle Pattern.
Advanced back-up — play the notes in each measure using the On/Off Pattern.

Shuffle Pattern

On/Off Pattern

Back-up Part

Improvised back-up — On your own, try making up a rhythm pattern and deciding what notes to play (choose from the printed notes, or talk with your teacher about using other chord tones).

Ideas for Improvisation

Improvisation is the process of creating music "on the spot," with the players making up notes or other musical ideas as they play along. In Celtic music, fiddlers often add *ornaments* (musical decorations like slides, trills, rolls, grace notes, etc.), or they may improvise variations to the melody or rhythm of a tune, and even more. But the tune is always recognizable.

Improvising is fun! Here are some ideas you can use as you begin to improvise.

Improvising with Ornaments

Ornaments—such as sliding the finger up into the notes, quickly played grace notes, rolls (or turns), trills, and others (ask your teacher!)—can make some tunes sound even more beautiful. See what happens to "The Minstrel Boy" when these ideas are added:

Improvising Bowings and Accents

Try changing the bowings by adding slurs, shuffle bowing patterns, accents, extra down bows, extra up bows, dynamics, and so forth. Using these ideas, "John Ryan's Polka" might sound like this:

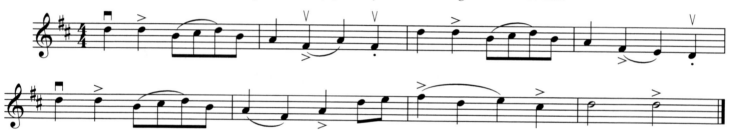

Improvising Rhythms

Try changing the rhythm of a tune as you play it. You can change the number of beats on each note, add rests, change rhythm patterns, and so forth. For instance, "Rakes of Mallow" might sound like this when you improvise rhythms:

Improvising by Changing the Melody

Another way to improvise is by adding notes—especially "neighboring" notes (that are just above or below the printed note)—and by filling in notes that are skipped when the printed melody leaps. You can also add double-stops and drones. By improvising on the melody, "The Girl I Left Behind Me" might sound like this:

There are many other ideas you can use to improvise. Ask your teacher to show you some more!

Remember the two most important rules of fiddling improvisation:

1. It doesn't matter what you play, so long as it sounds good!
2. Don't stop playing! Keep going! If you run out of improvisation ideas, just go back and play the tune itself.